W9-ARG-188

Withdrawn

JAN 0 6 2016

Northville District Library
212 W. Cady Street
Northville, MI 48167-1560

World's WEIRDEST Animals

Echidnas

Big Buddy Books

An Imprint of Abdo Publishing
abdopublishing.com

Marcia Zappa

abdopublishing.com

Published by Abdo Publishing, a division of ABDO, PO Box 398166, Minneapolis, Minnesota 55439. Copyright © 2016 by Abdo Consulting Group, Inc. International copyrights reserved in all countries. No part of this book may be reproduced in any form without written permission from the publisher. Big Buddy Books™ is a trademark and logo of Abdo Publishing.

Printed in the United States of America, North Mankato, Minnesota.
042015
092015

THIS BOOK CONTAINS
RECYCLED MATERIALS

Cover Photos: Tier Und Naturfotografie J und C Sohns/Getty Images; Shutterstock.com.
Interior Photos: ASSOCIATED PRESS (p. 15); Australia Zoo/Rex Features/AP Photo (p. 25); ©iStockphoto.com
      (pp. 9, 15); Arco/R. Kiedrowski/Glow Images (p. 29); Minden Pictures/AP Images (p. 19); D. Parer & E.
      Parer-Cook/Minden Pictures (pp. 17, 23); Shutterstock.com (pp. 7, 13, 30); Kristal Thomson/Taronga Zoo
      (p. 21); TUNS/Glow Images (p. 5); Dave Watts/npl/Minden Pictures (p. 27).

Coordinating Series Editor: Rochelle Baltzer
Contributing Editors: Megan M. Gunderson, Bridget O'Brien, Sarah Tieck
Graphic Design: Adam Craven

Library of Congress Cataloging-in-Publication Data

Zappa, Marcia, 1985- author.
  Echidnas / Marcia Zappa.
      pages cm. -- (World's weirdest animals)
  ISBN 978-1-62403-773-3
  1. Tachyglossidae--Juvenile literature. [1. Echidnas.] I. Title.
  QL737.M73Z37 2016
  599.2'9--dc23
                          2015004762

Contents

Wildly Weird!

The world is full of weird, wonderful animals. The echidna (ih-KIHD-nuh) is one of the world's only egg-laying **mammals**. It lives on the islands of Australia, Tasmania, and New Guinea.

Echidnas have long **beaks** that are **bald**. Their round bodies are covered in spines. All of these features make echidnas wildly weird!

Did You Know?

The platypus is the only other mammal that lays eggs. It also lives in Australia.

Echidnas can live more than 40 years in the wild.

Bold Bodies

An echidna has a round body and short legs. Its little face has small eyes and a long, thin **beak**.

Different types of echidnas vary in size. Adults can be 12 to 35 inches (30 to 90 cm) long. They weigh up to 35 pounds (16 kg).

Did You Know?

An echidna's small nose and mouth are at the end of its beak.

SPINE

BODY

EYE

BEAK

LEG

7

An echidna's body is covered in fur. The fur may be brown, black, or light colored.

The echidna's back, sides, and head also have sharp spines. These are light yellow, often with black tips. They grow about two inches (5 cm) long.

Echidnas in cold areas (*below*) tend to have longer, thicker fur than echidnas in warm areas. So, only the tips of their spines show. Echidnas in warm areas have shorter, thinner fur. So, more of each spine shows.

Where in the World?

There are two main types of echidnas. Short-beaked echidnas live on the islands of Australia, Tasmania, and New Guinea. Long-beaked echidnas live only on New Guinea.

Echidnas are found in many **habitats**. They live in mountains, deserts, and forests. They are also found in scrublands with small trees and shrubs.

Did You Know?

Short-beaked echidnas are usually smaller than long-beaked echidnas.

Europe

Asia

Africa

Pacific Ocean

New Guinea

Indian Ocean

Australia

= Echidna Region

N
W · E
S

Tasmania

An Echidna's Life

Echidnas live alone. But, their home areas often include shared land.

Echidnas can be active during the day or night. But, these animals do not like heat. So, they find cool places to rest when it is hot. These could be in hollow logs, under bushes, in caves, or in **burrows**.

Did You Know?

Sometimes, echidnas use burrows left behind by other animals. Other times, they dig their own burrows.

Echidnas are shy. They avoid contact with other animals and people.

Safety First

Echidnas have a few **predators**. Eagles, wild dogs, foxes, and Tasmanian devils hunt them.

An echidna's short legs make it a slow runner. But its long, strong claws make it an excellent digger!

When an echidna is scared, it digs straight down as fast as it can. In no time, only its spines are left showing. This makes it hard for a predator to pick it up.

On a hard surface, an echidna will curl up in a tight ball when it is scared. Only its spines will show.

15

Favorite Foods

Echidnas are also known as spiny anteaters. That is because ants are one of their favorite foods! They also eat beetles, worms, termites, and young insects called larvae.

Did You Know?

Echidnas use their beaks to find food. They have a powerful sense of smell.

16

Short-beaked echidnas mostly eat insects. Long-beaked echidnas (*below*) mostly eat worms.

Echidnas have long, sticky tongues. They can stick them out up to seven inches (18 cm)! Echidnas use their tongues to grab food.

An echidna doesn't have teeth. Instead, it has hard pads on the base of its tongue and the roof of its mouth. It uses these to crush its food.

Did You Know?

The long-beaked echidna has spikes on the front of its tongue. These hook food, such as worms, and pull it in.

An echidna can only open its mouth wide enough to stick out its tongue.

Mating Trains

Male echidnas work hard to win a **mate**. Once a year, up to ten males form a line behind a female. They follow her around. This is known as a mating train. Sometimes, they do this for up to a month!

The male who stays closest to the female the longest is the winner.

Echidna Eggs

Echidnas are a type of monotreme (MAH-nuh-treem). These are **mammals** that lay eggs.

A mother echidna lays her egg in a pouch on her belly. The pouch is not always there. It forms specially to hold her egg.

An echidna egg has strong, leathery skin. After about ten days, it **hatches**.

Did You Know?
Usually mother echidnas lay one egg at a time.

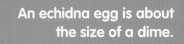

An echidna egg is about
the size of a dime.

23

Life Cycle

A baby echidna is called a puggle. A newly **hatched** puggle is smaller than a jelly bean. It has bare skin. It stays in its mother's pouch. It drinks her milk and grows.

A puggle uses its tiny claws to hold on to special hairs in its mother's pouch.

After about one and a half to three months, a puggle starts growing spines. So, its mother removes it from her pouch. After six to seven months, a young echidna stops drinking its mother's milk. It has fur and spines and can feed itself.

A mother echidna leaves her puggle in a well-hidden burrow while she looks for food.

World Wide Weird

Short-beaked echidnas are common. But, long-beaked echidnas are in danger of becoming **extinct**. Much of their **habitat** has been cleared. And, people hunt them.

It is important to know how our actions affect wild animals. Through change, we may be able to keep weird, wonderful animals such as echidnas around for years to come.

Did You Know?
There are laws that limit hunting echidnas.

Because echidnas move slowly, they are often killed by cars. So, drivers must watch out for them on roads.

FAST FACTS ABOUT:
Echidnas

Animal Type – mammal

Size – 12 to 35 inches (30 to 90 cm) long

Weight – up to 35 pounds (16 kg)

Habitat – mountains, deserts, forests, and scrublands on the islands of Australia, Tasmania, and New Guinea

Diet – ants, beetles, worms, termites, and larvae

What makes the echidna wildly weird?

It has a long, bald beak, its body is covered in spines, it digs to stay safe, it forms mating trains, and it is one of the only mammals that lays eggs!

Glossary

bald lacking a natural covering, such as hair or fur.

beak a stiff mouthpart that sticks out.

burrow an animal's underground home.

extinct no longer existing.

habitat a place where a living thing is naturally found.

hatch to be born from an egg.

mammal a member of a group of living beings. Mammals make milk to feed their babies and usually have hair or fur on their skin.

mate to join as a couple in order to reproduce, or have babies. A mate is a partner to join with in order to reproduce.

predator a person or animal that hunts and kills animals for food.

Websites

To learn more about World's Weirdest Animals, visit **booklinks.abdopublishing.com**. These links are routinely monitored and updated to provide the most current information available.

Index

NORTHVILLE DISTRICT LIBRARY

3 9082 13086 8469